Old BISHOPBRIGGS

by
Rhona Wilson

BISHOPBRIGGS FROM THE NORTH.

© Stenlake Publishing 1998
First published in the United Kingdom, 1998,
by Stenlake Publishing, Ochiltree Sawmill, The Lade,
Ochiltree, Ayrshire, KA18 2NX
Telephone / Fax: 01290 423114

ISBN 1 84033 054 6

Kirkintilloch Road, *c.*1906. The Triangle Shopping Centre, opened in 1991, brought dramatic changes to Bishopbriggs' nineteenth century town centre. Although the two large tenement blocks in the foreground on the extreme corners are still standing, most of the other buildings on the right have been demolished. Near the school, at the end of the road, Schoolfield Lane was swept away and slum houses known as 'the Diggings' became the site of the Safeway car park. The development was part of a much needed drive to improve shopping facilities; the following year Low Moss Retail Park opened with shops leased by companies such as Comet and B&Q. Although Bishopbriggs had to wait until the nineties for its shopping complex it has probably fared better than some other Scottish towns. Not everyone may approve of it, but it sits far more comfortably in the town than comparable projects of the 1960s.

INTRODUCTION

Bishopbriggs is first documented in Cadder Parish records of 1655, and according to one historian only had eleven residents in the mid-1700s. Even four centuries later, after substantial growth, the village was still being referred to in terms of its mother parish. 'Bishopbriggs', Neil Thomson stated in 1903, 'is the fast-growing capital of Cawder'. Despite fears that the village would end up being swamped by nearby Glasgow (swallowed up 'in the capacious maw of Auld St Mungo', as one local put it) its house-building programmes of the twentieth century, combined with its strong sense of identity, have ensured its survival. Instead it was the fate of Cadder, a gift from King William the Lion to the Bishop of Glasgow in 1180, to fall by the wayside, with 2,000 of its acres being donated to the city during the 1920s and 30s.

The derivation of the name Bishopbriggs has caused controversy over the years. Some prefer the explanation that it was named after 'the Bishop's Bridge', supposedly that over the Callie Burn near St Matthew's Church, whereas others believe the middle 'b' is a corruption. This, so the argument goes, appeared because it rolls off the tongue more easily than the original name of 'Bishop's Riggs'. In this alternative 'riggs' refers to the fields which the Bishop of Glasgow raised teinds (tithes) from. Whatever the truth of the matter, Cadder district was undoubtedly dominated by agriculture until the nineteenth century, its progress encouraged by the markets brought in reach by the Forth and Clyde Canal.

By 1793 'all farmers [were using] spades and barrows' and the introduction of fertiliser and better ploughs had improved yields. While crops such as oats, barley, potatoes and flax flourished, Cadder's population fared less well; a decrease of around 600 from the mid-1760s was attributed to new agricultural methods which combined smaller farms or run-rigs and swept away independent tenants. By 1836 there were 'almost no cottars' with the largest farms employing no more than ten or so, and some of those as maid servants. Land reclamation (through drainage) changed the landscape so that crops grew, 'where [once] the adder basked [and] the moon-fowl fed'. Dairy products, despatched to the Glasgow market, were relied upon to cover ground rents. The district's farmers claimed that the Ayrshire cows they bred had surpassed the original.

Development during the nineteenth century was slow compared to the industrial explosion of, say, nearby New Monkland Parish. In 1836 Bishopbriggs' population stood at 175, compared to neighbouring Auchinairn's 284. The missing factor was coal, but since this was brought to the village so cheaply by Bishopbriggs' excellent communication links (the canal, plus roads and railways) there was little incentive to invest in discovering it. Employment was instead provided by the district's freestone quarries. Bishopbriggs' train station, opened in 1842, underlined its status as the emerging focus of the parish although its expansion was slow and steady rather than dramatic; throughout the latter half of the nineteenth century the village population increased at the rate of approximately 100 heads per decade. By the end of the nineteenth century, however, the Carron Company (an iron and mining concern), was the district's main employer, building the hamlets of Mavis Valley and Jellyhill to accommodate its workers.

Heavy industry didn't fare for long, however, and Bishopbriggs suffered the decline shared by the rest of the country in the early decades of the twentieth century. Most of its quarries were worked out by about 1900 and what mines it had closed systematically throughout the 1920s. Luckily, manufacturing industries arrived after the First World War to soften the blow, with engineering firms, a wire rope factory and Blackie and Sons Publishers amongst those providing alternative employment. In the 1930s Bishopbriggs' emerged as an administrative centre for local government, although the final stage of its expansion was yet to come. The last major boost to its population came about as a result of the building programmes of the fifties and sixties which replaced Balmuildy and Woodhill farmlands with housing estates. A campaign by the local Ratepayers Association won Bishopbriggs its late bid for burgh status in 1964, the same organisation playing a major role in keeping it out of Glasgow district (and within Strathkelvin) during the local government reorganisation of the mid-70s.

These days Bishopbriggs is an attractive and flourishing small town, its village centre still recognisable from photographs of the early years of the century despite massive changes in the district as a whole. A population of c.21,000 in the early 1970s was a testimony to the building which left the west side of Kirkintilloch Road 'resembling one big housing scheme'. In the 1980s it was estimated that just 20% of these inhabitants worked in the town. A survey conducted by local churches in the late nineties concluded that it was 'a highly desirable commuter town . . . but losing its identity as a result'; 87% of the population rarely or never visited a neighbour. In the past the village was so close-knit that incomers were scared to talk about anyone according to one such interloper, since 'if ye spit on one, ye wet them a'. Certainly, Bishopbriggs has less of a parochial feel than Glasgow's other satellite towns but, by the same token, it is doubtful whether the burgh and district campaigns of the sixties and seventies – which did much to foster, as well as express, a sense of fraternity – would raise the same level of support today.

Auchinairn derives from the Gaelic *auch-an-earna* and means 'a field of barley'. Auchinairn Farm, north-east of the original Auchinairn settlement, was finally swept away in the late 1960s to make way for a housing development. In its past Auchinairn was inhabited, variously, by weavers, miners, railway workers and quarry workers, the latter group carving a living from the quarries around the Springfield lands which once separated Auchinairn from Bishopbriggs. Cadder Parish had many ancient links with Glasgow University and in the mid-eighteenth century Auchinairn Estate was owned by its Principal, Dr William Leechman. The tea-room on the left of this early 1930s postcard became Cameron's general store at one point; the site is now occupied by a glaziers although it's difficult to tell whether it's the same building. The tenements with outside stairs further up the road have been demolished.

Main Street Auchinairn during the early 1900s. Weir's Building, on the left, has since been replaced with modern housing known as Liddell's Court. To the right is the site of the present day Glen pub, next to Littlehill Golf Course. Auchinairn Estate was advertised for sale in 1838 at an auction in the Royal Exchange Sale Rooms in Glasgow. At this point the land was owned by a partnership (J. G. Campbell, Joseph Morrison and others) and it is possible that the estate had been acquired as a business investment. The notice of sale described it as 'an Estate near Glasgow, containing Ironstone and Coal'. Bores put down during the previous summer confirmed the presence of minerals but, for some reason, the partners decided to sell the 105 acres; it is possible that the coal was at too great a depth to recover economically. On the other hand, the advert suggested that the estate would make, 'a desirable, permanent residence for any Gentleman in business in the city'. By the middle of the century that gentleman was Thomas Leslie, and the land was also known as Leslie's Estate.

auchinairn village

Looking down Main Street towards the Tavern. On the right is the old Auchinairn school which became the local community education centre in the early 1970s. Dr Leechman, of Auchinairn Estate, left a bequest to help fund a school in 1764 on condition that children were taught 'literature and Christian knowledge'. Attendance was a problem at certain times of the year, as in other rural villages. In October 1896 almost half of the pupils in primary four and five, both girls and boys, were off to help harvest the potato crop. Four years later it was decided to redistribute part of the summer holidays to October to cover this period, which seemed to have a beneficial effect on attendance overall. The school in this picture had a residence attached for the headmaster which was burned down by idle schoolchildren some twenty-five years ago. The original school doorway remains although the building has been altered with a modern entrance added for the community centre in the late seventies. Auchinairn's new primary school opened in 1968.

Many buildings are still recognisable from this 1904 photograph of Auchinairn. To the left is the tenement named 'Helenslee' (carved into the stone at the side of the building), although no one is sure who it is named after. The wall beside it has since been knocked down and the land behind it is now part of the war memorial garden. During the world wars Bishopbriggs and Auchinairn were considered far safer places than industrial Glasgow and were chosen as destinations for evacuees. Both village schools were closed for a week in September 1939 to admit the young incomers; teachers emphasised the fact that it was a privilege to be involved in looking after these strangers to encourage their smooth integration. The cottage in the right foreground has been modernised.

The corner of Glendale Drive, *c*.1930, from a postcard captioned 'The New Houses, Auchinairn'. Old Auchinairn School was at the top of Auchinairn Road, as was Kinniburgh's piggery. It was apparently possible to stand at the top of the hill and watch the men playing quoits on the green below. One of Auchinairn's claims to fame is that the plague afflicted the village in 1666, soon after it arrived in London. It is not known whether this is true or not although disease was certainly a feature of life for many families before the twentieth century. In the early 1800s cholera broke out in the village and its victims were supposedly buried at Old Auchinairn in an area which was thereafter known as 'the tombs'. (It's possible, however, that this name refers to the private burial ground in Auchinairn, one of six in the parish.) The *Statistical Account* of 1836 mentioned the dysentery epidemic which had spread through Cadder Parish a decade earlier, killing old and young alike; it was considered a mercy that the young died quickly unlike adults who might suffer for a year before meeting their demise.

Kirkintilloch Road at Colston. Built around 1900, this tenement block at the junction with Hillcroft Terrace was mostly occupied by rail-workers, miners and quarry workers. In the past Bishopbriggs' freestone was much in demand for building in Glasgow and was apparently used to carve the two lions which guard 'Il Magnifico's' Mausoleum in Hamilton. By the turn of the century, both the parish's freestone and its whin rock (used for road building) was largely worked out, leaving the quarries as environmental hazards. In 1922 an attempt was made by James Macintosh to sue the district council after his seven year old son, Charles, drowned in a quarry near Cleddens Farm. The court ruled in the defendant's favour, saying in its judgement that the council had no obligations because the quarry was 50 yards from the main road. Over the years most of the old quarries were filled in, although they are still held responsible for much of the subsidence in the district.

Colston Terminus, photographed from Kirkintilloch Road on its first day of operation in October 1954. Today, a mixture of modern flats and waste ground have replaced the fields in the background. Trams first arrived in Bishopbriggs when Glasgow Corporation extended its service to the village in 1903. The journey, which ran across the city to Rouken Glen, was known as 'the red route'. In April 1922 the *Kirkintilloch Herald* reported complaints about traffic on the Kirkintilloch Road with a general feeling that there should be regulations about where exactly motor charabancs could stand. It was suggested that the tramway stopping place should be moved to a spot nearer Glasgow or, if this wasn't possible, that motors should be forced to wait at a distance of 50 yards from it.

BISHOPBRIGGS.

Kirkintilloch Road. Many villas were built in Colston during the 1920s by wealthy Springburn residents. Just opposite the horse and cart on the left is one such building which now houses Drs. Wilson and Keddie's surgery. East of Colston, across Crowhill Road, stands Hunterhill House where Thomas Muir lived with his family in the 1780s. An ardent reformer, Muir's political naivety condemned him to a role as the inspiration for change rather than the instigator of reforms. In the 1780s he left Glasgow University on a point of honour to finish his degree in Edinburgh, and was involved in a local dispute at Bishopbriggs, with the powerful landowner James Dunlop, in the early 1790s. His legal victory against Dunlop, who attempted to fill a ministerial election committee with his cronies, gave him considerable confidence. In 1792, together with William Skirving, he helped set up a system of Scottish reform clubs, their membership open to people of every class. Just one year later he was arrested for sedition after presenting a nationalistic address to the Scottish movement's general convention on behalf of the United Irishmen.

HUNTERSHILL HOUSE
BISHOPBRIGGS.

Muir's adventures had only just begun. His trial date was moved forward several months while he was visiting France and his non-attendance (it was difficult to travel from the country at that time) made him an outlaw. When he eventually returned to Britain in August 1793 he was sentenced to fourteen years transportation and shipped to Botany Bay on the *Surprise*. Whig donations meant he was able to buy a degree of freedom (from hard labour for a start) but in 1796 he decided to risk escape. An American ship took him to Boston from whence he boarded a Spanish ship bound for Monterry. Unfortunately he was arrested by the authorities and shipped to Havana, where he was considered to be a spy and packed off to Spain. During this latter journey his eyes were badly injured during a conflict with three British ships. In 1797 he was released by the Spanish government and chose to travel to France, where his political ideas had been acceptable in the past. He died in Chantilly two years later. In 1844 a monument was erected to him in Edinburgh. His family's estate has since been developed as an outdoor sports centre, but a room of Huntershill House has recently been converted into a museum.

Franciscan Convent, Kenmure, Bishopbriggs.

Kenmure House, now demolished, was situated near the fourth green of Bishopbriggs Golf Course. It was built in 1806 for the town's Stirling family to designs by David Hamilton. Charles Stirling sold the estate to his brother Archibald ten years later and it remained in Stirling ownership until the early 1860s. Towards the end of the nineteenth century it became a Franciscan Convent, the nuns running an 'approved school for girls'. Throughout the early years of the twentieth century parts of the estate were sold off for redevelopment as the golf course, a bowling green, the industrial school and housing. What remained was bought by the council and turned into a public park; local children had been using the driveway to the mansion (which later became Kenmure Avenue) as a play area for years.

KENMURE U.F. CHURCH. BISHOPBRIGGS.

A historian writing in 1903 commented that Bishopbriggs had only developed on the west side of Kirkintilloch Road up to that time, because the owner of the land was against feuing it out. Kenmure UF Church is still standing although it is no longer as isolated as it appears in this 1908 photograph. Today, the space in the background is taken up with modern Tudor-style housing.

Brackenbrae Road, *c.*1910. Although housing schemes were planned for Brackenbrae in the early years of the century, the First World War interrupted building and many of them date from the thirties instead.

MUNICIPAL BUILDINGS

BISHOPBRIGGS

Bishopbriggs Municipal Buildings were built to house the town's fire and police services *c.*1915, although the fire station later moved to its own premises in Hilton Road. Today, the original building is basically intact although the wall at the front has been replaced by a much lower one. Some of the police houses nearby have since been sold to private owners. Opposite the police station is the Crow Tavern which has a long history in Bishopbriggs, appearing under the same name on an 1896 map.

Arnold Avenue, Bishopbriggs

New housing has been built on the land at the end of Arnold Avenue. The large building at the end of the road on the left is now divided into Springfield Works Industrial Units, and some new buildings have appeared towards the end of the street on the right. During the construction of the nearby railway line in the 1840s a foreman, Joe Green, was killed by two of his workers. The culprits, Dennis Doolan and Patrick Redding, who lived in Paddy's Castle in Auchinairn at the time, stole his watch and valuables. Both men were sentenced to death by hanging and their accomplice was transported. The gallows were erected at Bearyards Farm, much to the chagrin of its owner Mr Warnock, because the site overlooked the scene of the crime. On protesting about the hangings being carried out on his land Mr Warnock was supposedly told that if he didn't watch his mouth the convicts would be strung up in his parlour.

Railway Station, Bishopbriggs.

This postcard was sent in August 1909 by someone who had got digs with the stationmaster, Mr Bennet, for a holiday in Bishopbriggs. The station opened as part of the Edinburgh to Glasgow main line in 1842 – in the beginning there was no bridge and locals had to brave the tracks to cross to either side. The railway company offered free travel to builders and this policy was eventually successful, with many villas being put in up in surrounding streets, such as Springfield Road, during the 1850s. Dr Beeching tried to close the station in the 1960s but the only things to go were the old station buildings; the village's valuable rail service operates to this day.

Bishopbriggs Bowling Green, laid out on part of the old Kenmure Estate, was opened by Captain Stirling of Keir and Cadder in 1906. There were other private clubs to compete with at Gartcosh, Stepps, Muirhead and Lenzie. Bishopbriggs' initial membership numbered 106 and the club is still flourishing today. The land that the bowling green occupies is currently leased from Caledonian Estates.

The War Memorial, Bishopbriggs.

486

Bishopbriggs' War Memorial was erected in 1920 on a site on the corner of Kenmure Avenue, donated by the district's powerful Stirling family. The memorial is still standing although its surroundings have changed greatly. The buildings behind it were cleared to make way for the Cross Court shopping complex in the early seventies.

20

Kenmure Avenue, c.1966. Bishopbriggs' War Memorial includes the names of several women who died in the town. One night in April 1941, just a few weeks after the Clydebank Blitz, approximately five bombs were dropped in the vicinity of South Crosshill Road. One fell behind Cadder Church Hall and another hit Mr and Mrs Hay's house (they were safe in their shelter). The blast of one of the last to fall in the road, however, hit the infants' school. At the time the high school comprised three buildings, and the infants' school was being used as the ARP's (Air Raid Patrols) First Aid Post. There were a total of seven fatalities amongst the women working in the school at the time. One was saved from shrapnel injuries because she had her fur coat draped over her legs for warmth. There seemed to be no particular reason for Bishopbriggs to be targeted; some believe that the bomber was aiming for the railway line, others that he was attracted by the white-painted school or simply had to unload his bombs before returning to his base.

The tram terminus was moved from Kirkintilloch Road to Kenmure Avenue in early 1940s although there had been discussions about resiting it as far back as the start of the First World War. The railway line in the background still provides a link to Glasgow.

RELIABLE SERIES 70.

MAIN STREET, BISHOPBRIGGS, GLASGOW.

Quin's public house, on the right hand side of Kirkintilloch Road in this Edwardian postcard, is still in business. Next door to Quins was M.B. Tennent's licensed grocers, run by Davy Johnson at one point.

Car Terminus and Kirkintilloch Road, Bishopbriggs.

Kirkintilloch Road, early 1930s. Near the entrance to Safeway's is a wishing well to collect money for charity. In the past Cadder Parish had many springs and wells although water from some of them was considered unfit for human consumption. Church records state that the minister had the free use of a well at Gateside, near the old Glasgow to Edinburgh Road. There was a public well on Bishopbriggs' Main Street and Auchinairn had its 'Tollen's Well'. There was also Cockplay Well (south of the Auchinloch to Glasgow road) and Muckcroft and Burnbrae Wells. In 1807 Bedlay Well was the cause of a dispute when there was an attempt to stop the people of Chryston using it, even thought they had been doing so for 40 years.

Bishopbriggs.
Lanarkshire.

The Commercial Bank, on the corner of Kenmure Avenue, opened in 1902. Charles Stirling set up one of Bishopbriggs' first banks in the 1820s. The intention was to give a 1% advantage over other banks, and although Stirling's bank was open to any Cadder parishioner, the writer of the *New Statistical Account* complained that it wasn't being used by the people of modest means who most needed it. It was thought that the bank would replace the system of friendly societies which the working classes used to guard against sickness or unemployment before the advent of the Welfare State. Things seem to have turned full circle since in 1998 plans to set up a community credit union were mooted by the Neighbourhood Forum. The Commercial Bank subsequently became part of the Royal Bank of Scotland, a branch of which still occupies the site.

Kirkintilloch Road, *c.*1905. In 1922 the *Kirkintilloch Herald* printed a story telling of a delay in supplying gas for cooking in new houses in Bishopbriggs. Glasgow Corporation refused to have the supply connected until it was paid for installing gas mains by the district committee of the Lower Ward of Lanarkshire, which represented Bishopbriggs. The committee insisted it had no funds to pay the £13 necessary for each household, nor even the 50% contribution which was suggested as a compromise. As a result, around 48 homes had no gas for two months.

Kirkintilloch Road, sixty years later. Kenmure Cinema, which seated over a thousand, opened at the corner of what is now Churchill Way in 1938. In December 1940 George Formby and Phyllis Calvert appeared in 'Let George Do It', Spencer Tracey and Hedy Lamarr in 'I Take This Woman' and Clark Gable, Joan Crawford and Peter Lorre in 'Strange Cargo'. As well as being sources of entertainment cinemas were also the only way to view newsreels (and hence war propaganda) before the advent of television.

Kirkintilloch Road, mid-1960s. Preparations were made in Bishopbriggs in anticipation of the outbreak of World War II in 1939. In September 1938 gas masks were distributed to schools and in February the following year the Auchinairn school attendance officer was asked to carry out a survey of housing stock for a potential evacuation scheme. When war broke out Bishopbriggs School was closed for two weeks to enrol 46 evacuees. Air Raid Posts were set up within the first few weeks and the 'blackout' policy implemented. A fair amount of effort went into constructing bomb shelters, even in the early days, such as the much maligned Anderson's Shelter which could be half buried in a garden but was considered unsightly. Food prices were set in September 1939 and ration cards were issued the following month.

Bishopbriggs School, described by Neil Thomson in 1903 as 'the most picturesque educational edifice in the whole parish of Cadder' was opened in 1896. It replaced the Old Stirling School which had been established through the financial assistance of Charles Stirling's widow and her brother-in-law. The new school could accommodate 420 scholars but an annexe still had to be added in 1928. Towards the end of the sixties Bishopbriggs' burgeoning population necessitated the building of a larger school. This was built on a site behind the old one, which was converted into the new library and opened in March 1969.

ALLAN GLEN'S SCHOOL CLUB. BISHOPBRIGGS

Allan Glen's School, of Glasgow, bought nine acres of land in Bishopbriggs for use as playing fields in 1922. Although the school had an excellent reputation for sports it didn't have its own grounds. Its Old Boys Club was expected to raise 50% of the costs and several large subscriptions had been received by the time the sale was reported in November's *Kirkintilloch Herald*. A bazaar was held in Glasgow's McLellan Galleries in December to raise further funds. The school club and playing fields are still intact today.

St Mary's Boys School is believed to have been built as an 'industrial school' and to have stood on the old Kenmure Estate.

GAWDER ROAD, BISHOPBRIGGS.

Although captioned Cadder Road, this picture and the one opposite are believed to show Kirkintilloch Road. Pretty Cadder has an ancient and weighty history. Its lands were gifted to the Bishop of Glasgow in 1180 by William the Lion and the parish had links with the University of Glasgow throughout the centuries; in 1507, for example, its vicarage was annexed to the university. Soon after it was presented to the bishop, Cadder was feued to Sir Alexander Stirling, whose family retained interests in the parish for over 700 years. After the Reformation the parish was acquired by the Hamilton and Kilmarnock families who transferred it back to Glasgow University in the mid-seventeenth century. In 1690 both Cadder and Monkland Parishes took advantage of an Act of Parliament which allowed them to opt out of the university's patronage which meant that the heritors and kirk elders then became the electors of the parish ministers.

Unfortunately, the law which allowed this change of authority and responsibility did not define clearly what a heritor was and this led to many disputes within Cadder Parish over who could vote to elect a minister. When Cadder Church needed to appoint a new minister during the 1740s the position ended up remaining vacant for about two years because agreement couldn't be reached over who was on the election committee. Similarly, when the *Statistical Account of Scotland* was written *c.*1793 the position had once again been vacant for two years. After the last clergyman had died in the early 1790s a dispute ensued between the elders (who had a joint say in the selection of the new minister) and James Dunlop of Garnskirk, a local landowner used to getting his own way. Dunlop tried to fill the joint committee with his supporters but found himself up against Thomas Muir, who insisted that their qualifications as heritors should be investigated on behalf of the elders. The Court of Session later found in Muir's favour; Dunlop also lost an appeal to the Synod of Glasgow.

Cadder Road, looking towards the canal. Although the haystacks would look out of place today, the old primary school on the left (now the church hall) is still standing, albeit minus its bell tower. This was used to sound air raid warnings during the world wars but has since been removed. The Kemp family's cottage, across the road from the school, has survived too. Before Cadder School was built the parish schoolmaster taught children in a barn in summer and the pupils' homes during winter. There was a schoolmaster in the area from 1688 although the financial provision accorded him often left a lot to be desired; Cadder's heritors were guilty of letting teachers such as William Stirling, master in the late seventeenth century, struggle by on meagre wages. Writing c.1793, William Barclay, a schoolmaster himself, stated that an attempt to improve schoolmasters' conditions by law had failed some time ago. The move had been opposed by some gentlemen who believed that '[their servants] would be more obedient and dutiful, were they more ignorant and had no education'. The first part of Cadder School was built c.1780 with two classrooms and a kitchen added towards the end of the century. Although there were only 23 pupils on its roll when it closed in 1980 there were strong local protests.

Cadder Smiddy was built on Cadder Road, near the canal, some time after 1875. This picture shows it c.1908 when farming was still largely unmechanised and tractors were yet to replace horses. Agriculture diminished in importance throughout the twentieth century; whereas in 1920 there were 31 working farms in the district, in 1948 that number had fallen to 24 and by 1989 there were only 13 left. Land became an increasingly valuable commodity with builders falling over themselves to buy it up for development. Private and local authority building began in earnest after the First World War with over 800 new houses put up by 1952. Just before the World War II there were plans to develop Cadder as a 3,000 acre 'garden city'. Professor Abercrombie of the University College of London laid down plans for this in 1936 but by the 1950s just 26 bungalows had been completed.

Old Mill, Cadder Estate. The 'Bishop's Mill' is referred to in records dating back to the thirteenth century. In the early decades of that century the Bishop of Glasgow granted one third of his Cadder lands to a certain Joanna (wife of David Olyford) but, because of a local dispute, took back this gift in exchange for the mill and its attendant privileges. This wasn't such a poor swap as it sounds because mills were once immensely lucrative. Farmers were bound to take their grain to the parish mill and had to pay dues there, often making the miller an unpopular character. This mill was built in the 1780s. Its lease was advertised for sale in the *Glasgow Courier* in July 1832, and it is thought that it closed some time between 1924 and 1944.

CADDER BRIDGE

Cadder Mill House was occupied until recently but since becoming vacant has quickly become a target for vandals. Although a Forth and Clyde Canal was proposed in 1723, the idea didn't become a reality for over 60 years. The aim was to link the towns of the west with the east coast and so improve communications, trade and commerce. Excavation began in 1768, with the crossing of the Dullatur Bog posing one of the biggest problem for the engineers. Finally, after changes of plan which included siting the western terminus at Bowling instead of Dalmuir, the canal opened in 1790, having cost over double the original estimates. Goods traffic was important to its prosperity throughout the nineteenth century with the 'track' boats (cargo vessels towed by horses) being the first to convey the products and fuels of the Industrial Revolution: coal, pig iron and timber. Passenger services were run by the canal company until the mid-nineteenth century and by private operators until the 1870s. Threats to the canal in the twentieth century began with the closure of the Forth ports during World War I and continued with the Depression, competition from road transport and the rising costs of fuel and wages. In the late forties it was taken over by the British Transport Commission. Parliament took the decision to close the canal to through traffic in 1963.

The *Gipsy Queen* was unusually tall in the water and was described when she was launched as 'looking like a giant wedding cake'. It was James Aitken, whose father had skippered the *Rockvilla Castle*, who revived passenger services on the canal. He launched his 'Queens' fleet with *Fairy Queen* in 1893, running day trips between Port Dundas and Craigmarloch. By the time the *Gipsy Queen* was introduced in 1905 the vessels, which combined private functions with regular sailings, had become a local institution. They weren't immune to competition, however, and when motor buses were introduced (during the twenties) Aitken found that he had to incorporate links with buses into his sailings in order to hold on to his custom. The *Gipsy Queen* began to fail during the inter-war years. She made her last journey from Craigmarloch to Bowling in June 1940 and, from there, was taken to Dalmuir to be broken up.

Canal boats, like this heavily-laden lighter, were originally towed by horses. Early passenger boats operated much like stage-coaches. The horses were changed every four or eight miles to maintain speeds, and were supplied at first by innkeepers along the route until the canal bought its own to improve efficiency. The first passenger boats took about twelve hours to travel the 25 miles from Port Dundas to Camelon although the journey time had improved to five-and-a-half hours by 1809. The Swifts of the 1830s were so called because of their ability to reach speeds of up to eight miles an hour. They were towed by two thoroughbreds, the first of which was driven by a boy riding the second horse. Canal horses got three days rest during the week on account of the gruelling journeys they made whilst on duty. The treatment of horses was of significant concern to the Glasgow and West of Scotland SPCA which patrolled the canals in the 1860s. The commonest problems were sores on horses' backs or shoulders due, usually, to them being handled by inexperienced drivers. Accidents such as tow ropes snapping could result in the horse being thrown into the canal with little chance of getting out again. The kerb visible on the outside edge of the path in this picture gave the horse a guide to prevent it from falling into the canal. Horse-drawn passenger services disappeared in the 1860s but cargo boats continued to be towed in this way until the 1940s.

The *May Queen* near Cadder. Although the canal closed to traffic in 1963, enthusiasts used it for regattas, fishing competitions and other recreational activities. In the 1980s passenger services were revived at Kirkintilloch by canal enthusiasts, who were overjoyed when the Forth and Clyde and Union Canals were chosen as a Millennium project in the 1990s, the aim being to have them fully reopened by Easter 2001. The biggest engineering problem associated with the canal's restoration is the creation of a new interchange at Falkirk. This has been designed as the world's first wheel-like boat lift. It will replace the eleven locks which were abandoned in the 1930s. A funding shortfall threatened to scupper the project's chances but an eleventh hour deal saved the day. An estimated 4,150 full-time jobs will be created by the scheme which is hoped to regenerate the canal corridor for tourist, industrial and commercial uses.

Cadder House, old residence of the Stirling family, was built *c*.1654. John Knox supposedly delivered the sacrament in the castle which was its predecessor. Most of the building dates to the seventeenth century although additions have been made over the centuries. The west wing was built in 1816 to the designs of David Hamilton. Wilderness Plantation, which covered its grounds, was planted to resemble the lines of battle at the Battle of Dettigen and described by Thomson as, 'One of nature's grand cathedrals, pillared with tall and stately forest monarchs'. An A-listed building, Cadder House was given a new lease of life in the 1930s when it became the clubhouse of the Cawder Golf Course. During World War II a large part of the golf course was used to grow vegetables as part of the 'Dig for Victory' scheme. It took many years to restore it to its former glory, but today it is truly magnificent. The circular stone doocot which was once used to supply fresh meat (in the form of pigeons) in winter still stands near the house.

Cadder Kirk. The name Cadder derives from the Gaelic *coille dobhar* meaning 'wood by the water or stream' which is an apt description of this scene. Alternative early spellings of the name included 'Chader' or 'Kaders' and there is still no unanimous agreement about whether Cadder or Cawder is the correct version. A church has stood on this site for 800 years, although the present building dates only from the 1820s. Its predecessor stood just 70 years, described by Watt as 'as mean a building as could be cheaply erected'. It had a clay floor and a leaking roof, a lethal combination when it rained. The church photographed here was renovated in 1908 (using funds raised by the congregation and the archaic-sounding 'heritors') and the structure shows some evidence of rebuilding. Cadder was apparently popular with body-snatchers on account of it being near to Glasgow University, and a watch-house still stands in the graveyard. Nearby, an ancient mort-safe, a cast iron coffin cover which was used to protect fresh graves from 'the Resurrection Men', lies in the grass.

CAWDER KIRK.

In the *New Statistical Account* for Cadder Parish, written in 1836, the writer, the local minister, complained about the state of his manse. 'No repairs will ever make it comfortable', he assured his readers, obviously fishing for some new accommodation. It's lucky he wasn't born a couple of centuries earlier because an incumbent of the late sixteenth century, Rev. John Bell, was banned from rebuilding his ruinous manse and ordered by the Synod of Glasgow to instead take up residence in the church steeple. Bell adhered to his superiors' request but this didn't stop them from 'disposing' him in 1611 on account of his Presbyterian sympathies. At the time religion was heavily intertwined with politics; Rev. Gavin Hamilton suffered a similar fate in 1649 for failing to promote family worship during the time of Puritanism whereas Rev. Thomas Melville was removed from office for holding conventicles. William Forbes, his eventual successor, supposedly lost his curacy for standing on the other side of the political fence when he travelled to Fenwick to help suspend Rev. William Guthrie for his covenanting principles.

The River Kelvin, pictured here at the stepping stones, could wreak havoc on the district's farms. Flooding caused great damage at seed and harvest times and William Muir's poem, *Kelvin Keep Low,* was inspired by farmers' losses. In the late eighteenth century landowners on the north side of the river built a series of drains and embankments in an attempt to control potential floods. The writer of the *Statistical Account of Scotland* didn't think much of this, feeling instead that they should have tackled the problem at its source by straightening and widening the bed of the river. Although the stepping stones provide a short cut between Balmore and Cadder they are vulnerable to displacement during storms and are often covered with water. Cadder and Baldernock Parishes discussed the possibility of building a bridge here in the early 1900s because the stones were in disrepair. In the distance in this photograph lies Balmore village, built on the line of the Antonine Wall, built by the Romans to contain the Picts. Remains of a Roman bridge near Cadder fort were discovered during the dredging of the Kelvin in 1941.

MAVIS VALLEY

Mavis Valley, known as 'the Valey', was a mining village built by the Carron Company to house its workers at the Cadder pit. It is thought that it was named after the mavis birds (song-thrushes) which populated the nearby Wilderness Plantation. Building began in the area in the mid-nineteenth century, the primitive houses arranged in two rows. These older houses had outside wash-houses with six privy middens at the end of each row. In 1901 89 two-apartment houses were built which housed 428 people. By the 1950s only 24 remained, occupied mainly by squatters. The rows of nearby Jellyhill, a corruption of the Gaelic *sheileach hill* meaning 'place of sauchs' (willows), were demolished in 1936.

A fire at Cadder No. 15 Pit (above) in August 1913 resulted in 22 deaths, devastating the local community. 26 men were underground on the Sunday back shift when fire was discovered at 8 p.m. The first stage of the rescue attempt involved reversing the ventilation airflow so that fresh air was drawn into the pit behind the rescue party; this had the effect of sending smoke along a connecting tunnel between pits Nos. 15 and 17, alerting three brushers in the tunnel to the disaster. They were Robert Dunbar, Felix O'Neil and Michael Keenan, and this probably saved their lives. Once the disaster was announced relatives travelled to Cadder from Lambhill, Maryhill, Shettleston and Tollcross, congregating at the pit-head, some 'reduced to a demented condition', as they waited for news. Of those who died thirteen were married with families. Charles Riley, who perished when he went back to warn his workmates, left seven children. Dr Miller of Bishopbriggs was on duty at the pit for fourteen hours; the poisonous fumes were so strong that some of the rescuers needed medical treatment.

Fire Fighters ready to descend No 15. Pit. Cadder, where 22 men lost their lives, on Sunday Aug: 3rd 1913.

3.

Pub. by
Walter. Benton & Co,
Glasgow.

To the astonishment of his rescuers, 28-year-old Michael McDonald was found unconscious but alive on Monday morning. Lying with his face down in the earth, his hands covering his nose and mouth, he had managed to escape the fate of his colleagues, the nearest of whom lay dead just twelve yards away. Following the disaster there was much criticism of the Lanarkshire Coalmasters' Association for their failure to organise rescue brigades. In 1911 the Coal Mines Act required mine-owners to establish trained rescue brigades throughout the country as soon as they possibly could. Over a year later the only service in Scotland was based 60 miles away at Cowdenbeath; it took eight hours to reach the scene of the disaster. 'It seems incredible,' stated the *Manchester Guardian*, 'that amongst all the collieries that cluster close about Glasgow, no such brigade could be found.' The industry claimed that the delay in setting up brigades was due to discussions with the Home Office on the type of appliances necessary.

Kirkintilloch Road, 1919. In 1903 Neil Thomson assured his readers that 'there is not a road . . . so kind to the old and frail, as this Kirkintilloch Road, and, in due season, the footpath is generally bordered with a rich profusion of golden cups and saucers bursting into bloom'. In the past part of Kirkintilloch Road was known as Moss Road on account of it crossing the High Moss. During the early nineteenth century it had a bad reputation for murders and highway robberies. Campsie farmers used to travel to the Glasgow market in groups for protection and there is a legend that, on one occasion, one who lagged behind had to defend himself from an assailant with a black pudding. In 1923 one wag at the *Kirkintilloch Herald* could not resist passing comment on the efforts of the 'motionless' workmen widening the road towards Bishopbriggs; 'once – and only once – I perceived a man using his shovel vigorously, feverishly – but that was to dig himself out and doesn't count. [Workmen] are good at leaving for home!' In 1950 the Stone of Destiny spent one night in a garage in Bishopbriggs after it was taken from Westminster Abbey by Scottish nationalists.